The Price of Light

Also by Pimone Triplett:

Ruining the Picture, 1998

The Price of Light

poems

PIMONE TRIPLETT

Four Way Books
New York City

Distributed by
University Press of New England
Hanover and London

Editorial Office
Four Way Books
POB 535, Village Station
New York, NY 10014
www.fourwaybooks.com

Library of Congress Catalogue Card Number: 2004101053

ISBN 1-884800-62-9

Cover art: *Provincetown Cemetery* by Donald Beal
By permission of the artist.

Cover design by Pablo A. Medina for Cubanica

This book is manufactured in the United States of America and printed on acid-free paper.

Four Way Books is a not-for-profit organization. We are grateful for the assistance we receive from individual donors, foundations, and government arts agencies.

Distributed by University Press of New England
One Court Street, Lebanon, NH 03766

Funding for the Levis Poetry Prize was provided in part by a generous donation in memory of John J. Wilson.

ACKNOWLEDGMENTS

Grateful acknowledgments go to the editors of the following magazines in which poems included in this volume, sometimes in different versions, have appeared:

Agni: "Narcissus to the Aquarium Guide"

American Literary Review: "Double Life" and "Lighthouse And Keeper, 1886"

New England Review: "Past Light," "To My Cousin in Bangkok, Age 16," "A Vision of St. Clare," "Bird of Paradise Aubade With Bangkok Etching Over the Bed," "Spleen" and "His Sepulchre in Two Voices"

Paris Review: Sections 2 and 3 of the poem entitled "Hive in Four Parts" were originally published in this magazine under the title "One More Time."

Pequod: "Hippocampus"

Poetry: "More Scenes From a Body" and "Ignis Fatuus"

Triquarterly: "Late Century, Long Drive With Stutter" and "As Of Two Ancestors, 1845"

Yale Review: "Guide"

"To My Cousin In Bangkok, Age 16" and "Bird of Paradise Aubade With Bangkok Etching Over the Bed" appeared in *Asian American Poets: The Next Generation*, edited by Victoria Chang with an introduction by Marilyn Chin (University of Illinois, 2004).

For all their support, guidance and friendship, I would like to thank Nicole Cuddeback, Shari Huhndorf, Robyn Schiff, Nick Twemlow, and C. Dale Young. My thanks go to Michael Collier, Mark Doty and Ed Hirsch for their encouragement and votes of confidence. Many thanks to Martha Rhodes for her commitment and patience. Much heartfelt appreciation goes to Rick Barot, who reads with passion and an eagle eye. And, once again, endless thanks to Corey Marks, for his vision and loyalty to the word.

Above all, I owe a special debt of gratitude to David St. John for selecting this book.

For Andrew

CONTENTS

I

Double Life

Since I'm not one with
the pitbull wind come down from the mountain parking lot,
the jay's thumping of seed pod on power line today,
nor the spirit of surf
rushing up from the off ramp out near cemetery road,

since there is no one mirror-name for the creek bed stoved with beer cans,
            t-shirt, shopping cart,
maybe it's best to let a *we* inside the chatter
     of *he/she/it* go ambient as

the day's imbroglio of light leaving by slow degrees.
Meantime, something pools at the edges when seen from above.
And if I come late on the scene, knowing blood
at the temples of 5 o'clockers sitting
         in traffic, travelling the longest vowel honk
in this the hour of Civics, Saturns, out-sized Rivieras,
maybe it's a case of how what passes

for drama of the mind is half machine, half dopamine
etching the brain's cracked mosiac,
     acronyms for lunar modules or photos
via satellite of farms clotted with trailers and fog,
of Dari Marts in the staggered hills
torquing a mist they make, the consonant bells tinkling
         as we go in, as we go out.
    And who wouldn't like to label *true*
any bit that sustains, including the peach
you reach for as the miles click by, a flood
of juice that makes the breath draw back,
       flesh of sugar water and sulfur-root,
the cloud ripened velvet horse neck slipping down

your wrist as you spin the wheel.
Your mouth making for the hieroglyphic
rock of the pit. And soon, the gravestones
come up quick off Route 109, don't they,
each one for sale, looking now nub, now gnome,
now angel. Little bids
for the soul-in-shape, stuck like any
constellation
among the carbolic stars...

And since I am not one, as I was saying, nor whole
of late, having suffered my belief to crumple under,
having tried to marry, by turns,
a bottle, a brother, a fancy, all the *he*
there was to hold
winced in time out the other side...
As for the myth of ancestors, my father
comes from a shack in the West, my mother
from a palace in the East. I say something
in the flesh sounds
like rain's sudden percussive way of telling, yes,
little one, the roof's still on.
Listen, I know a woman
who gets down on her knees
in front of the hall closet
checking towels for loose threads, for evidence,
spittle, signs of liquid voices, ghosts of her fathers
coming on fathers, and forever coming on...
Listen, I'm a woman who gets down on her knees
when I pull over to this rickety bridge

for my face borne up in the brown water again,
breeze garlanding its bit up the middle.

Stray leaf.
Algae in swirl. Smell of ocean nearby. Clay
and spit

                 raked from the mudbank
just reflective enough to give anyone
       their *you*   and *you*

as if come down also to lift, to say   *this life*, double
or nothing—a flick of salt and you're lucked

                       along.

Guide

after Beato Angelico

Out of the glorious before, out of the sleeping year 5,000,
you go into the forest spilling many among the one.
Take Armor. Take your Primary colors of Paint.

      And if you're chosen, pick bare skin for outfit
over others. Climb inside the bone lintel, nerve stream,
the one style, mostly strumpet, of face, and stay

easy as you lift that velvet hem of threshold.
There's water to be bloodied by and by.
Also, the shadows lacquered, the sugared grooves,

        infinite square roots, the best tongue
and veins—as you get it, backlit, your body—
the single shape of fire, forged to hold.

Happens then, always: the restlessness
that enters, crashing like any bad guest.
You could be king, slave, wife, a banker of nations,

      a dwarf to the court. If you tire of trysts
in the mirror, go barefoot into the walls
of the city, slowly unsandling your pride. Friend,

beware High Windows, the Bright Wheel, the carpet
of cats' eyes in back alleys, moving
all the time away. As for the nouns,

        the names, they're for you to live
through: bent swords, stone patrons, smell
of cabbage, the burnt marrow stew.

At the end, when you want me, you should
sleep six days in the bottom of a well.
No food or drink. No man or woman. Careful,

in this time, your own skull-to-mouth soundings.
They can crack the mind, your little mosaic of chutzpa,
life-house, loose sand. Trust me. Hand that once did

can lift, sort, stitch, but you must ask, now and again:
please. Drops on the same rock, the snow, rain.
You spin the alphabet on air, in between.

Story For the Mother Tongue

Bangkok to Chang Mai

Went to see the *there* that was, for me, full
latitudes, umpteen tracks of world away.
On a train, as it happened, sputtering-to-brake
half our time up the country's question mark coast,
feeling beneath my feet a churn of steam and tin can,
hiss of dithyramb, bike spoke, whole gutter balls
in the aluminum beast. A full car hummed
with that one tongue not mine, but almost.
Since it was my own aunt, after all, who sang
out from the platform that morning not to be
kidnapped—*lukpa*—by anyone, nor taken
into the jungle for who knows what.
And so I knew a little of this music, falsetto
bounce and stutter up from the lungs of my mother
often enough. It came to nothing against
that din in the aisles, boxes and loose seat straps
jostling, the rise and fall pitch of two kids wrestling
their plastic bags, curry-slick. A boy beside me,
teen-aged, kept coughing the way
a kitchen timer ratchets backwards.
He fed his dog mangoes clumped in sugar
and red pepper, the cage rapping for miles
on the window smear of rust and whiskey light.

Until finally something happened so that this couldn't
be the one about the exotic anymore, but instead
I had to brace myself as the train lurched forward,
suddenly stopped. And how standing in line
for the bathroom the boy pushed himself into me
then, put his hand hard on my chest, high I don't
know, booze on his breath maybe, I don't know.

I couldn't get free when he whispered into my ear
in English *jesus christ* and then *slut*, his lips moving
slow like words he'd just learned, like reciting after
the teacher in class.

                    Later alone in the WC at last,
gray waves of florescent power buzzing off, then on,
then off again, one fist-sized window, one way to look out,
I stared down, awful batter in the hole, a grid
near the feet grinding one blackness up against
another. Longer I stared the more I could feel
space shrinking all around, the crowd of us skimming
the river of tracks we rode on and no still point
in any of us by then, I thought, the water running
with no quiet under the blood and tissue, face and bone,
door jammed, and then just sounds bouncing in the small box—
the two syllables—*kap khun*. Which in Thai means
person, though I thought it was *please* when they
came from out of me at last, words I must have made
while pounding on the walls just then—*kap khun*—locked
in place, the seconds breaking open, mine
and endless and the train moving slowly on.

As of Two Ancestors, 1845

Story goes, cattle fattened, the wheels in rut,
goods borrowed or bought on credit, the bulk ready,
she slipped from staggered hides down the wagon
packed to hosannas, breaking an arm,
so it was decided he should go on without her.
Home-bound then, the joint set in haste,
elbow throbbing always part of her to hostage,
she started the chiseling of instances, her ledger
of staying in place. Each thing mirroring
the mind alone, she'd keep track, try
to memorize the moments beyond
the garden weeding up all season, the plot
of dirt bricking below a lack of rain. Days,
wanting to see deeper into, say, the paper wasp
riding unseen waves in sage bush, or the lop-
sided columbine's snarl of petals dropped
in heat, she wrote the record he could
come home to. At night, checking her own
face reflected, warped wide in the mantle's
urns of ash—his mother, his father—
she waited to hear, trying to listen hard
within the fire's crack of falling
back on itself: stubborn, moldering,
stirred by chimney's lesser wind.

Meanwhile, head bent to a breeze scanning
the broad plain, his mind moving, truing its brocade out in the elsewhere.

Back a stitch to her now,
then forth into the forward, a turning and turning, always about to complete.

Not sleeping, not wanting
the day's end, orchestral, echo of bats, their screech and round, a rough

hum of gnats
in swarm above him. Evenings, out to overtake the end, straddle what he couldn't

see, there, behind the two-tiered stack
of tree line half-hatched out of the mist it makes: the forest's

final catacomb, the secret
starting up from a story. Restless, he wrote her how, not far from the rock face

where he'd carved their name,
the mule, after braying for hours, gave out–a sound of steel grated live in the lungs,

followed by long quiet.
Hunting, he said, most days, wolf skins for county wages, out westering, still

looking for the right
spot, a new home—*it's possible*, he kept repeating, *for free*. In his mind a dream of dirt

piled in straight lines,
long doors unhinging his one desire, below the beds of sand, silt, worm, water,

lay a perfect dark: land, its sprawl
and secret, all the furrows a winged plow could portal into....

Then upwards she saw the end: snow wrapped
as a cast binding beech limb, red oak, linden.
Having wintered long enough in his absence,
one night she emptied out the urns.

His mother, his father. Wrote down
how first she let their bodies'
chunks and rubbish fall
into an empty bucket, then fed
all his letters to the fire.
Later, she walked away from the house
cradling the ash and grit
of her missings in the small tin pail.
Kneeling to the ground then, she put her hands
into the mix, smeared some onto her chest,
more onto her lips. Flung half
into the air, half into the waiting
dirt. After that, she put palm
to cold cheek to colder stone,
lay down as if the frozen
ground could hold her.

Ignis Fatuus

Comes in flames easy to mistake,
fool or *fox fire, will o' the wisp,*
complete with once-upon's to fill out
what isn't, *friar's lamp* and *corpse candle,*
this afterlight of gases no one can agree on.
In marshland the purple or blue-red clouds
wick up, pure motion hitched to random
methane molecule. I've seen them rise
faint as any good intention
from the solid ground, half as likely
to blow out. And whenever I catch that glow
in the distance I can also see the man who is not
my father, although he is still young enough
to look like his hope. The black soil out there
is firm as the moment he feels himself
to be in, driving alone, hands sewn
to the wheel. He's seen the lights before
and so pretends he doesn't. He's had enough
of here again, gone again, feeling small
against the brilliance come up in gusts.
Say it's 1967 and he's on his way to a bar
with decent music, a tender who minds
his own business. And the bog-fill slides
by in secret, the flashes sweep along side
windows of the old Corvair, until all he wants
is the smoke squared in tonight, held tight
under the sooty oak ceiling, floored
by a little jukebox and booze. Just the night
he'd like to enter over and over, but getting it
right this time, a night of slipped decision,
the flashes in dark now simply store-bought
match fire, that low rhythm and blues

buffing the wooden walls. The war still on.
See how he reads the letter from his wife
now, fingering the table's sticky grid
of ashes, the sloshed beer worked in,
as if to press the words firmer into their places—
duty, accident—to stop their burning, her final
coming to you. Happens, she's on her way
back from the other side of the world, Bangkok
and the land she comes from which he can't
start to imagine. So that when he drops the page,
rushes to the phone, it's only to say *no,*
to burn the story, the romance, in reverse, set
the fuse hissing miles back into some kind
of freedom. And I can't get enough
when he tells me again how he saw and didn't see
the room back then lit with its small
luster—glass glint, a wall-eyed roam
of headlights pulling up, jukebox blink and glare.
Until the call is placed, of course, and doesn't
get through, the war still on remember. For a few
instants, his decision sits badly rigged
on some switchboard that he sees in his mind
to this day, the pin prick lights marching
red, white, purple, blue. Like a flag,
he thinks, striking a match to see the number
again, the operator saying again *no, I'm sorry sir,*
and the flag flying, little grid of all our lives,
the second chances shutting down, everything
turning on a dime. Even though the man's
ten stalled minutes lead to only minor
disaster, a bad marriage, the years' little
skein and buckle. Even though there's a child

who might have been erased, who wants
to stand forever now in the first memory she has,
holding the man's hand when he takes her past
the town limits, past sunset, to see the ignis fatuus,
the flames with a name like an animal
getting away or light glowing like a fever
you have to ride forever before it breaks.

Spleen

Let's hear it for spleen, for how it survives
nine times ninety-seven lives, rutting in
all that's stubborn—the gene pool, elephant's
ass, dirt's secret deal with a fossil,
the fat boy whose bat it is. Spleen, ever
moving, nursed on the tits of a troll under
a bridge, reared in heat smashed to infinite
paw prints, the cougar pacing its cage. Here's
to the full stadium, the beer jockey
selling spleen, making his way down the rows,
remembering his deadbeat dad. There's
a girl in the ladies', third stall from right,
spelling out spleen with her own blood, tracing
the graffiti couplings of others. And as

for my spleen I say it's pure of heart.
I've let it grow all alone, a potted
plant in the dark, eating dust, old dish suds,
coffee grinds, cracked-at-the-half egg shells.
With river's mud I've tucked each and every
leaf into my body's first idea. What
else could pump me this wild with fury
and focus, this morning's vision of the one
who tried to steal my car keys, honor, candle, soul.
My enemy's been sighted, he's huffing
and puffing, he's riding a pricey tricycle
through traffic. Spleen says what's mine is yours
and his. Together we drive all night, break
into his house to shave all our secret
spots with his new razors so he'll never
know why his day is that much
duller. Memory's long for me and my spleen.

So give us back whole histories boxed
in the basement, jars of pennies, glass eyes,
plastic pearls, all the kid's leftover life-glut,
we can't waste a thing. Once I heard someone
say a body doesn't need a spleen. O
sanguine us not, dear rage, blessed bile, but
keep us long in the pain put there to make
us move—dear Spleen, keep us steady,
keel us past the reasons.

Last Score
Robert Schumann, 1856

1.

So that all day he's stared the mountain down
its myth of windowsill, followed by, live, sight
of an oak shaking as a fever into leaf, alone

                              to make the crooked straight

and later was kind to Nurse but took no food,
lest the poison come by spoonfuls, as he must keep

                              ongoing the metronome

precise in how he takes the room in, careful
how he pays attention. And if the light bulks up
above, storming, another summer in asylum,

                              time and again

he whistles softly to himself, getting it right
by halves, his mission of hands set

                              mid arc, listening,

trying to find the chord and then the shape
inside it. As for the hours, always
that drip from the corner basin,

                              cuffed to storm and scherzo

the A note arriving low at his inner
ear. By night he's heard the way a branch

trills its signature up
the rough bark, wrapped around
what amounts to need.

2.

Could have been a dream, the wholeness, to own
time's stretch and scatterstone again. Some
twenty years old, his hands still infant to discipline,
the days new-bred and everything going in major.
Always Clara playing downstairs. They competed
for hours. For practice, he built his own
design, lifting the finger by pulley and sling,
clamping his right hand, the weak one,
in pine and awkward irons, steel pins,
silk cording, anything to flex perfection
into the flesh. Still his good invention, his small
stab of will. After the bone and tendons,
made brittle, broke through, crippling
the limb for the rest of his life, she came
to him one night as if for the first time. Lay down
beside him, humming, the whole notes held,
as she put his damage to her lips,
snuffed the candle out.

3.

Then one day the worse than nothing—
piano eating its one note, a wild quiet,

into him. Making him pound away until

by evening he's strapped

to each minute and having to keep
the scream down as they push

the upright out from under him

so that he's mouthing, *no*, and *thank you, but he's had better*,
then shouting, *no*, and *he can't play anyway without the brace.*
He thinks, after they gag and leave him

go ahead, take

the wood and wire casing, the strung
hammers. What they can't know:

how she'll come

any day now and he'll stop
the starving, begin to drink wine
from her fingers, he'll show them all

the crooked made straight.

They'll see now how wind
plays the rain in lines, how it can be strung

all motion, the mind

and its quiet culling a way in,
de crescendo, as the door is pried open
and she does come in,

                                  her hand stretched out

until he lays down to listen at last
to that music, having grown so wholly

                                instrument.

Without: Migration

If not for the geese, wild scar
on sky, black with ash gray,
barking their lift, re-settle,
brief stay, for weeks and then

not (until the corner turned
one evening was all
their blue air loud with lack)
how to think,

this slowly a wound
might close? How else to find
the downy upper-part
of grief had slipped off. When

and when. Blood thickened within,
en route beyond the hollow bone.
As written in their wings
always the *must* that made

for this vectoring out, invisible.
For a long time one wakes
and would rather not. Facts: your
flesh underground, the way sun

laid its veil or feathered grace
or simple grid over your place, just
before the dirt was shoveled in.
And let's admit won't I miss

you less and less, friend, or with
difference? Look up, in flight,
the necks taut as arrows, a shape
reduced, as you loved,

to mere direction. Dear salt bed,
worm grit, suffer us unto
the laws of light. Dear daystart,
cradle us in between,
the little that winters over.

His Sepulchre in Two Voices

God if you get me out of this rib-gripping empty
        for a couple of days I swear
I'll be good in this middle earth of yours

                all wet with blood, bright

Cause after the centuries' haul and fresco
        couldn't I love the world
a little, caught though I am ever beneath the moment

              after he's risen, before he's seen

As I would be anything other, would sing
        like a girl I saw once
striding by, laundry in her arms, thinking of

              his body taken

just a boyfriend maybe somewhere in the electric hills
        inside her head, spun and dusted
bright gold, lifted up, dancing a little in the breeze

              splendor

And I am wholly weary to be still
        your best blank, Lord,
barren as the dry sand, side of a cliff

              you must wait until

And yes I've trembled to great blessings,
        father, to know the son,
to feel his skin quicken, the pulse begin

time flaps open, a flag

waking to stand straight up. The land
        to the left slipping winter,
land to the right coming spring. All the while

a flat horizon, his spine

a line of epic to split this rot, God, from that
        rigor. But where's the warmth
I felt then, his blood pouring back, a king

his hem not to touch dividing

risen straight as a tree? Since when I said
        "him" what I meant was
the instant just before this one that keeps

justice

sifting away. Stutter step of breath's
        edge, the always,
that's also a trace of although

that relic

Tell me why they smashed my stone darkly
        into shards, ground
quartz and sand, halving me open to gravel

mother rock

Why live, why marble, why color of flesh,
       why made,
why hold, why dust, why ending in edge

                   more luck

Please picture me over again, I'd be
       the river in shallow, clean,
clear to see through, light as your touch again

                   to contain

II

Bird of Paradise Aubade With Bangkok Etching Over the Bed

        Woke to hear you refuse
to stop working in heavy rain, shoveling the mud
that beggars our part
                of the yard. After a while, I heard the rasp of iron's
rake on gravel, wet earth, your bending for the gaps
to get the seedlings right. Then for hours from the window

        I watched all your muscles connecting up, your body's parse
of sweat and salt, hollows
between the ribs appearing, then not, around your
                breath's steady reed and thrum. Watched,
you see, until I knew, for once, I wouldn't try to leave.
Though I did want to walk out and say something else

        about moving through the myth
of ask and answer once. I wanted to tell you how I saw it spill
out on sidewalk, alleyway, underpass, and how traveling
                that way, in another country,
I had to love the hawkers' come ons,
their peddling, every night, the Leda and swan-style

        tracings. On our wall now, I can make out her limbs
misted in chalk blear, the thighs streaked, but still skirting his will.
And when you come in I want to show you
                the half man, half bird, the one whose mouth
hangs open, his little razor-cut hungering of how much
he wants her. Or have you see the way a span

        of white rivers between
them, the distance of missing they wed again
and again. The chalk drifts through
                the design. Outside, a real bird's rapid trill in flight
skirts the window frame. And now you're stepping over
the lawn's dropped

branches, carrying the tallest stalks still hung with weeds.
Getting there, you say, giving me the ones almost in bloom.
After you turn away
                              I put the buds to my mouth
to taste the skin before it breaks open, the bodies, newly green,
bound to root-pact, stem-line, moments before they fall.

Past Light

Within reach of sex but not yet, I remember, a few stars
        freckling the vacancies
past the yard's blown flood beams and father's single
        sycamore. Expert amateur,
I thought myself, aged thirteen, rabid for facts and trying
        to have a mind for
what each light was. This I knew: arrivals of gaseous crackups
        wholly unlike us, and not
pinpricks, nor quaint connect-the-dots, nor tiny stabs of will.
        Sky's Zenith, Lyra, The Great, The Small Bear.
Hopes rose. It was before the boys and window escapes,
        before breakup seeped
into the house like bad water. I loved stories
        of staying in place.
In the one about the ancient astronomer
        on the day of eclipse,
after he'd gazed his naked sight away,
        he thought he saw the sun giving birth
to itself and scrawled, half blind, in a notebook,
        as if wood fought back
to eat the fire. Meanwhile, our lawn sparked
        with mother's rake tines upraised,
sound of door slam and squabble inside, squeal
        of brakes rounding
out the drive. And if I wanted one clean,
        one lesser loyalty, wishing
so hard on that old onlooker?
        I could see him at full kneel
in dirt unflinching, begging the above to smote what's bulk,
        the words arcing slowly up,
saying, *burn me all to star, o fathers.*
        I understood nothing of their pain.

Already, close to home, the sycamore leaves in full
heat looked edgeless,
each dark on dark blurring the shapes
as though we all dropped through:
Zenith, Lyra, The Greater, The Lesser, The True.

A Vision of St. Clare

Girl for whom the job came as a crack in rockface, the sudden
        tomb-slip turned all door.

So that when she saw the lily spell itself there, seraphed on the wall
        of her father's house, she knelt

down for the rapture, the rupture, and started to dig. Wall through
        which the dead in those days

were carried for burial, delivered into, they prayed, His secrets
        held deeper than dirt.

On the night of the rock loosening beneath her fingers to gravel,
        to seconds falling ordinary

as hourglass, the little sands cinch-waisted, Palm Sunday, in Assisi,
        in the family house,

1212 A.D., she listened to the mice scurry and flirt in the hallway, then
        to the one dove's sound

of silken pebbles tumbling in its throat. Turns out later they asked,
        for what, the mother and father,

getting up for the scream, running to find her there in rubble, blood
        rivering steep down her arms

by then, instant the wall fell, and first light entered, and she stepped
        clean through.

The Price of Light

1. Merit Ceremony

When Uncle paid for holy men by the unit,
        two dozen a day, plus
candles and chants and incense, all
        in the name of not being
wholly ignored by the gods, for weeks
        and for luck,
we finger-set the gold leaf squares against
        each gazebo rail
in the yard. Gardeners for hire too, spaded up,
        dead center, the best
royal shadings: fire-red begonias, ochre scrambled-
        egg trees, refills
for the lily pond, plenty of roots, he said, to snag
        a blessing's eye.
Also, there was hope that our "passed on"
        could pass back
to us somehow for a single day/hour/second,
        some bit from beyond
this life's governing grids. Meaning
        his wife, we guessed.
The one whose death stumped the doctors,
        flesh leaving her inch
by inch as she thinned, until we could see clear
        through her skin, light
leaking in from behind her joints, the ears and elbows
        day-flooded,
luminescent if she held up her hand. Uncle counted
        out the right sum—
a hundred gold statues, food for the monks,
        one huge mirror so the glint

could be seen from above. Past the skyscrapered
        sky, our top-knotted temples,
a strip of land, the family of lowered heads, each
        bowed as a closed bud, shining.

2. National Bureau of Economic Research

This lead chapter leaps across, as progress,
the skewed head of history, breaking new ground
for the hunt. Today's bulb creates around
ten thousand times what homo erectus
put out in caves, waving his flame on a stick.
Theory tells us how tracking light's story
shows the present, at first, as less costly
than we'd imagined. Paleolithic
man struggled mightily to scrape a lamp
from limestone. Indeed, real wages must be
re-figured. The first gas globes, fittingly,
by comparison, pale. All these attempts
factor past the truth, that achilles' heel.
Later, some genius finds fire in a whale.

3. Phuket FantaSea

Meanwhile there's kudos for cross-pollination and plastic
kinaree, for every be-spangled bird/woman, lion/man,
the national costume hook-and-eyed by now

       to happy greeters spawning
gold wing fake outs—these barkers, relentless,
       birthed teak-slim and girlish

into this life. Theme park, the sea. *Elephants fed,*
buffet all kind. Plus mother-of-pearl spittoons for sale,
a toddler palming air inside the bargaining big tent.

       And if the spirit of the land
is hawking freeze-dried
       durian for export and iron-on t-shirts,

selling teacups, neon-blinkered toy kites, each plying flight
and remembrance and *I was here*, then why not?
Idea being, deep inside the darkened cave, the princess

       still gets saved by laser show each night,
as something half-blooded this way comes. The sacred
       Tiger, touched by magic wand poof,

pads down the hidden door. Also a lone chicken,
hybrid breed, lost in the act,
blindly wanders the stage.

4. Imaginary Homeland

All summer she hummed above the plank of pills.
She stacked her medicine to face the east,
and that equatorial sunlight ate its way
over dust peaks she couldn't really see—aunt they called
crazy lady, lost crone. Waving the first finger
I was afraid of, its refusal to wear the flesh
simply, the knuckle swollen, arthritic, a tree knot
dead center at joint. *You know*, she'd joke, *I'll live
"dalord bai"— forever.* Time she showed me
the white, yellow, blue, to her, as bouquet centers,
measures spilt from pre-sepia'd plastic,
she'd already hacked them with her small knife.
I watched her swallow slowly, purposefully,
as if she wanted to feel each small weight
of how, by then, even the doctors would do
what she wanted. Her throat's glide inside
the neck creased like cold pudding skin.
                              But if a mist
drifts through the scene, eye's afterimage
and dim lineage, I swear I've got it right
about that one time she ran out wild
with migraine in her nightgown. Everyone
laughing in the yard, the mowers roaring
on and off and on again that day. How she stood
in the doorway and waved a kitchen knife,
held it high over her head until the sun
caught there gleaming. Then pressed
the blade hard to her own lips—that glint
and shush enough to quiet, to quicken, us all.

5. Phi Phi Island Cave Tour

Darling, I wish you could have been here. The cave mouth came so close to our faces we had to dip way back over the boat's edge, like dancing. Plus each of us piled up in this logjam not wanting out of the alcove. The pool gone green 'cause of daylight coming in from underneath. A color like that absinthe you smuggled in once, plus floating patches of key lime. In the end all of it streaming in, we thought, from star to sternum, to find us.

&

Imperial blue   gives way to fat black struts,

spot where rising rust   makes a top hat of stone.

You can see the lime   takes its time dripping bone-

shaped columns its own   weight couldn't take free

                              standing

Inside, counted bats   hung from slats, stalactites,

man-faced, as last light   blinkered by. Cave hush stung

us. Would you believe   a wild peace, as if lungs

found first breath among   our bodies, pillowing

                      in circles, our each....

&

Then ink-dark, shark dark, shadow. Dark of belly seed, bull's eye, baby's mouth. Velvet dark, bamboo, dirt dark, ash. Forgotten box dark, dust dark, black of your great aunt's attic. Spleen dark, heart dark, liver dark, down to root-rot dark plus never to let slide by, dark grave.

6. Shrine

Later I was taken to the river bank
where once upon a time the most valued
body in the kingdom gave way to water.

When the Imperial barge capsized
the King's favorite, the most beautiful
Queen, with the unborn child inside her,

drowned. No one at fault. Maids and helpers
tossed overboard also but forbidden
to rescue, as a royal is never to be touched.

Instead they tread beside her in the weak tea waves
as the mother, half goddess, in her heavy robes,
sunk under pocks of sunlight working the surface.

Now on dry land, photos and candles piled altar
high. What's *put in place*: chrome, magnesium
melt for the face that stays, marigolds

for the soul that doesn't. In each picture,
beneath her high forehead, the soft boned look
of a woman already elsewhere at the marrow.

7. Queen Saranthai (b. 1888. d. 1903)

From here, uttering again old world
bespeaks edge-lure, *fat*
already
         and *paid out*. End came as curse,

of course, solid mass: the silk, once spun raw,
my divine right, soaked fast through.

        All to marry
skin's more and more
impossible heft. Besides there were

        handmaidens, there were stunned
eunuchs nearby.
From birth, not to touch.
So the age bloomed us up,
        wishes

royal as orchid, purple as plush.

        As for the child
inside, the would-be king: never
plot-spanked,

never end-of-tunnel struck.
        Not breaking womb swaddle, from
amniot float straight to slow dissolve,

river's wet caress
        simply the new surround.
And maybe day world, rude

ark-light, flashed by his mind
like a dream. What sun there was flung
           honey white, a sheet

hung above the crowned
           all round bassinet. Not that I could
touch him, beyond that first belly scrawl

of blood. Clean translation
he is now and worth the price of perfect.
His always not crying, his ever spared
                          from air.

8. As If Incant

And if gnashing's all epicure of us

And if portion knows old holidays of ache

Sing past the code, past star-in-a-mist

Tell me the starting sum,
what luxuries eddy
out of blood

Did you say you'd come
Recollect quiver, sally forth what's starved

Of course I'd like to mention home

Which is to say *earliest day-scud* and also
suture me out of here

Later we learned Uncle spent all he had

Someone calls to inform us lonely again, sick again

Neither I-loved-you-more-than,
nor would you
please erase these squalls-on-rockface

And still the theme is sea

Please come

Lacy jags of acre,
our glaciers of sorry inside of
arrival

Are you willing to change your name
Can you start with amoeba, *that* first dance

Chronicles tell, my love,
how fire spoke for once,
a cave inside a cave

All to show us to us
in shadow huddled over
bone-crumb,
driblets of blood

but priced dearly,
betrothed to banquet,

palm to palm new pressed
over the heart

Did you say you'd come
Please come

Someone still reads from the book of stone

After this, there is only subtraction
You have to take it whole,

minus the price of light

Oystering

Today, touched the inside gone alabaster,
under the sea fruit and waves, this curve
of pure unearthly soap, plus the spot,
glazed mahogany, where the heart
must have held on. And I drove all afternoon
to see the oyster beds from this bridge,
their small geographies, sunken tea leaves,
where the wet jewels grow strung to wooden
sticks before someone cuts them for harvest.
As for the story I carry in my hip pocket,
the one about the saint who worried how long
the present could ever hold true,
past and future slicing the hard blades in,
maybe I should mention how I've come
for the bridge itself as well and the *now*
that's sweeping beneath by way of wind's
light harangue on bay water. Or tell how
the men who once worked the mud flats,
their backs bent to weed clusters in searing
cold, were fathers, uncles, brothers, sons,
some of them mine. So that drops from the family
blood line leaked, now and then, I suppose
into low tide, hands, wrists razored open
on the sharper shells. All for the muscle
within, the edible almost eye.

                       In those days,
they let the younger kids out from school in time
for gravity, its local tug on water miles, the moon
and ocean floor becoming everybody's something
to count on. Pennies paid by the full flat only.
And when I look out today, they've got mountains

of cast-off casings in the parking lot and beyond,
horizon's merely the least best seen
of borders. A redwing blackbird heads
for the dock now like a notion coming
into focus. Somewhere I want to say to the boy
who gets out of this town, the one that goes on
to become the man who makes up half of my birth:
don't give me any ordinary secret. Wasn't there
a brass and marrow music you clung to
inside your head, arms stretched out for the wooden
load sled, wild symphonies, string quartets
you saved before the radio got sold?
The blades slicing in from both sides. Maybe
you could tell me about the membrane's
slow dissolve clear down to the ocean floor.
Since I want the muscle, the hidden skin
that's close kin to secretion, and held in its two
cupped lunar landscapes, this mix of rock,
chalk, fingernail, papier-mâché, dimpled
to make these caves, which by a lesser fate,
a gull's tongue might tunnel into. Some of the pleats
filled with sand. Some of the dirt never lifting clean.
Though there's no saying any of this really.
There's only the oysters to eat tonight, each one
tender as a mind loosed from its little skull, sliding
down my throat, giving the world's ooze
that for now is edgeless, gray, cold, and blind.

Patron in the Painting

Browser, suffer me, dust me from
fat oils, designs, these lines laid
rich, all our faces centered
as navels. Long ago, the dates
in ledger stained and razed,
my best finery over-thumbed
by year one, the canvas halved
once during summer, cracked
by oafs. Now I can feel the limits
even to air, spun upper right,
the master beleaguered that day
by scant supply of blue. Still,
lucky I was back then to pay
my way in lengthwise. Others
tried the same trade-off, a few
coffers for lasting past
maggots. But my torso,
for balance, fit most fine,
they said, and soon the novices
copied and mottled, brushed
me once by velvet, twice by all
deemed fair for some demi-god
called Composition. I stood, stand
still, in stocking feet, held in the *hold*
he named, little schemer, with
flourish: our *thresh*. Not bad,
since I see you well enough
where the edges bisect. What I
wouldn't pay to give a glint
as you do moving across
the museum floor. All your sidelongs,
seconds, paved together,

coming in sneakered step
from the gift shop, change
in your pocket. To plunge in looks
easy, to ride the eye cone, breath
stream, whole zones of *this* then *this*
before the slip outside, a face
in scattered sunlight you can own.
But please look past me.
Back there, always the one
in charge, son-of-god, elbowing
the ordinary mosaic into myth, gazing
up and over the little spit-shine histories....

About to be cut down, risen up, whipped
clean—for what? Just this moment
made monumental, and no forward
for the frame but for the far you—
the axis, the million-eyed, turning
away—a point that can only vanish.

From Seaside After Switching Between Stations Praise! and CNN
for C. and A., who couldn't come

So you see I came here anyway
zoned strip behind the country's
junk
squatting in carparks,
of Real Estate and Aqua World

unclean)
old pals, spot you couldn't
this time by tragedy
flights cancelled, headlines
steel speeding down from the sky)

I walked what seemed
glass and gravel before
and the mile you'd like most:
arrow)
God,

you could have made it, if only to see
limpet try its other look in air
just-a-rock
Because when I crouched to see past
where the prehistoric plates overlap

bloomed like a flower, like a movie)
the sea urchin's pale cervix
I started thinking, friends,
just discovered, between you, inside
the womb walls and tissue and

fluke of cells
of the great deep rise)
by now *(the thousands gone)*

all along the no-
glut of shore
its happy trash and meals, dumpsters
the azure-fat promises
(now the land was

And I've studied the place pretty good,
get to, sideswiped
(the bringing of floodwaters)
(glittering
Early today

a long while over broken
I got to low tide
the lesser *(a flaming*
life that's half-hidden under water
I wish

the ribbed
a deadpan getting by as
(the severe clear called in)
the profile of sun, no-sun
(someone said the fire

and caught
spun open for sun,
of the child,
(all the springs)
suddenly it felt like no

(though waves
but a crowd
and maybe mine

coming along
Then turning back to shore

could still see billboards' gills
plying their bargains for better
(whenever rainbow) vision. Opposite,
smack in the scene's middle, the bluff, pollocked
with gull guava, holds, we know by now,

the minnows' apparitional glimmer
on maze *(someone)* on match-struck
coral *(waving a t-shirt,* *a white flag)*
So tell me, after I ran past the two birds going at it,
blow by blow, feeding

in pinches on the still live fish flailing,
scales flicked all around how we teach
anyone to take on the damage *(as everything,*
or mostly will perish) saying here and here is
the terrain: heartbeat and rock's edge, lung flush and

blood's little epoch in the chest Plus out there
horizon's line *(where ships* *have sunk, will sink)* a curve
the eye can't count or say to them *(soul)* come down.
(In the beginning) millions walked out of the sea
holding their bits of the wreck tenderly

III

Late Century, Long Drive With Stutter

Each time I look out following
       the storms of snow roadside,
the headlights have at it, a slice of white
       rivening the proximities. Both hands
on the wheel, I try it slow. Everywhere a scuttling
       of particles (no two alike) seconds before
I drive the whole spinning thinness to disappear.
       Meanwhile, voices on the radio
sputter up bits of the stories, the shootings
       and bombs on target again,
more madmen, someone just said (at tether's end).
       I can hear about the ones forced to stay
and the ones forced to flee. But when some mile
       or mountain pass makes the girl's cries go
static for me, I lose that daughter
       weeping through war and bad translation,
telling how they wanted us for *who we were*.
       Can't say when the small shame sets in,
this not being able to listen anyway as the atrocities,
       all too familiar, the far off cruelties
go abstract, the girl hard to hold. Outside,
       (a swirl) snow's up in arms, until I can't see
its filching of the visible.

           Although I remember
       (pulling over) how once I thought I heard inside it,
something huddled under the distances.
       Heard it happen to—with—a stranger. I was
a child, at home. Came in the night, this rip,

the sudden almost whistle note waking us—
was it a teakettle—was it a siren—? Then everyone
          running through the hallway to find it, father, mother,
me, each of us hearing in our turn
          no, it's a scream (lock myself inside now).
Someone back then opening the front door
          (snow, that flurry outside), and then her
falling into us. She a *she* all *red*, I thought, then
          no, all blood—blood running with a face behind it.
Her scramble and scrittering into the corner.
          Each of us trying to do something, trying to find
the right thing to do (windows steaming up now).
          Can remember mother at the phone,
father checking outside (the white on white,
          a swirl) and me on the floor with her face.

Her jacket flapping blood and glass,
          her arms around me, gripping, the storm
of her still screaming, rising up at me
          (starting to stick), then the room
bleaching white, all the lights coming on until
          I saw it from above suddenly, each of us
locked inside, spinning out, the different directions,
          each of us hurt, but her more so, sliced open
somewhere—where? the opening, her wound
          was where?—Each of us a privacy scraped wild,
and my wanting her off me by then (I admit),
          for her to shut up now anything but this
fear gone full throttle up from the voice and guts of her.
          Soon I heard further within maybe
(no two alike), something blank, sickening—no
          core at the core—no pulse and spin

under the skin, all her quiet
        deafening in the little hall—*(And I let*

her go.) Later the police came, pieced
        in the details, how she'd been kidnapped, car-jacked, forced
(the long drive). How he'd laid her down in lawn
        after lawn (a red on white). And now in the distance
horizon's nothing, gone slipshod, smudge,
        and I get the snow in dribbed bits
off the interstate. A crackle and I get
        the voices back on, updates on the updates, whirling
(and the listening deep enough is?). She lived
        in the end, thank god, on her way out kept
stuttering up from the stretcher: he was just a kid,
        he was a child, she tried, he wouldn't
listen (and the *is* inside the *is*
        is?) And if I open the door
this very second, climb down
        into the gully, cup the cold flakes
in my hands, couldn't it be only
        for the melting, the stillness, that finishes—
I catch a quick blinding
        up from the ice bank outside,
then the squall shot surface, disturbed, circling.

To My Cousin in Bangkok, Age 16

What space is for, to the boy peddling
through smoke and traffic blast,
past curry stalls and lean-to yard
encampments, is to keep in place
the dreams of the dead. Each night
his mother, long gone, appears to him
with the same command, saying *get up,*
go out, take the ride now, so that mornings
he snakes across the city to the old house
that was once theirs. Out to tend what little
remains from her life among the living,
he comes crashing through last year's
pile of peach and lychee cans, wrappers
bleared by heat below the carport, and goes
inside to dust the table's one blue bowl.
He shoves his fingers down into the fuchsia
broken open beside the windowsill, moves
the tv from porch to den and back again,
trying to remember what she wanted.
It takes all day to work these increments
of an intimate geography he'd like,
just once, to get right. Because there is always

behind him, you see, the one time he didn't.
Night his mother lay dying, he beside the bed,
there's the moment when she stopped
shaking and he made his first mistake,
thinking *now she'll be all right*. As she went
cold he covered her body with more blankets,
so she could sleep, and after that he left.
How the room might have darkened then,
small bed filling with that new weight.
And now if he comes back, fills the bowl

on her table with clear water, gauging
its cold for a second in this house
where he was born, the one she gave him,
it's to test his bit of the absolute, plunging
his hands, almost a man's, into the blue.

Whether to Marry

Coming in through car windows: salt
air, breath-text, edgeless. Also all along
the farms, barns, billboards and graffiti,
our props upstaging the actors, missing
for miles. You could say, look how nothing
needs us, our chatter and plans passing
through day's end, the sundown
streaming its buttered light on every
weather-backed beam and shingle.

> *So sing to me, Love: sundial on fire.*
> *Gather me umpteen mazurkas*
> *in leaf bud, in secret, in petals*
> *small as mice teeth. Tell me*
> *how to pour the right notes*
> *into your svelte, your velvet*
> *ear.*

Or take that flock of sea terns,
flashing, almost see-through, coming by
syncopate, spin and fast break—all together
in flight until, one past the many, a single
body gets away. Sky lead gray with sudden
wing flick. And later what to make of it,
when he comes flying back into formation
and they are *they* again, getting it
right, their slip and minglings,
a veil visible, then not, as we're gone.

> *Or maybe it's like the one about the princess*
> *who tells anyone who's willing, go ahead,*
> *take it, meaning, remember, the boxes.*
> *Everything in threes, the lead and silver,*
> *the promise of gold. Idea being: if*
> *her picture lies inside your choice, you can have her.*

Headed home, late, searching the shallow
roadside, I get the usual plastic bags, nothing but
the wrapper-ridden earth, Love, plus,
in bits, the wild columbine's skirts
flirting the gravel edge, a little
pinkening of innards it owns.

> Tell me ditched inside the secret, a dare.
> Repeat after me, daily I do unto
> more days, in sickness and in health,
> the throat's hum and straddle
> of calendars, whole arias of if's and then's.
> I say yes to the ride's yellow dash lines,
> blackberry's avalanche on
> sewer pipe and wet cement.
> Yes to sudden apple cores
> tonguing this gully part of the way,
> hero's profile at the wheel all along....

If I touch your hand, it's to feel
your pulse and undering gone
instrument, how at your fingertips,
knuckles, palm to palm and wrists,
lies the *here* and *here*,
how day drives into you
that much more
to exist.

Grief Hotline

Take days you wake thirsting all the way through,
past soul, if there is one, dry spackled in the guts, past
mood or duty or get up at all, pretty sure heart's
       flickering in there somewhere,
a box inside a box humming in the name
of no one.
              Then you stretch your hand
to the window and start to touch day's first light
driven along the splintered frame, its canyons
       for ants, dust mites, beads of wet on the glass
where suddenly you wish you could tip your tongue
and drink for hours. Which is when you try again to think
of the one friend you've got who can least
       afford to disappear.
                  Since he's out there,
manning his post at one end of the Grief
Hotline for the State of Blank, and you're lying
in bed still dry in the throat
       remembering how once he told you
about going into the field for a girl. She lived
in her car off Highway 9, refused
to let go of the baby who'd died. So he drove
       out to where he was supposed to, over
the freeways and mesas and red cliffs, their look
of marbled steaks broiled up on horizon.
             He said she didn't move when he got inside.
       Years later he'd think of her black hair
petaled back as from a center that's had it,
her thin arms spooling from her flowered blouse,
and the way she kept staring through the car window at the few
saguaros holding their water for years.
           And he didn't know what to say then or why
he finally started to sing. Or hum, really, a low glide

in the throat. But soon it became notes close to *twinkle
little star*, or the one for the alphabet,
                              a tune with no ending,
and he kept going though for hours she wouldn't
look at him or move.

          By nightfall, something in his nursery chant,
or the way his chest lifted and fell with breath and silly
song to steady them both, or the notes sounding split
from their little caskets of word and word, he couldn't say
          what worked or finally told her
to set the bundle on the seat beside him, but she opened
the car door and walked out to the stand of three saguaros
                              as if to find some new shape to hold. Which
is also the spot where she disappeared
from your friend's view, coming to you second-hand after all
so that you have to get by with no story to this story.
          Only the notes
and the words he didn't say,
that other river, in secret, underneath
                    the rest of the noise.
And this is what you try to remember and how
you sit up and swing your legs out of bed
and walk across the floor,
flooded with your things to do
          in the hours that you're given,
human and thirsty and willing to listen to anything.

Hive in Four Parts

1. Last Days of First Marriage

At the end of the Book of Change,
when the square of *he* plus *she*,
　　　　infinitely divisible,
gets written over and over again,
　　　　　　　factor in the small room they shared,
and how she asked him,
　　　　once, to trap the live bees under glass.
　　　　　　　To capture and not to kill.
All morning from behind the window frame—some hole,
　　　　a zero they couldn't find—
came one then another small invader.
　　　　Until she made him put an ear
　　　　　　　right up to the edge,
hearing the yellow jacket gyrating
　　　　its small rage inside the vase, the drone's
oil-to-hot-pan buzz
and struggle. Before that,
　　　　of course, his stalking the prey,
Prince of the kingdom, poised.

2. Spending the Night

Tired of the tally of give and take,
until (worth it at last) I found your store
past the nickle and diming phases of dance.
I'd like to stay, ready to be leveled off.
Chance led us to better rates, fair exchange,
luck far off the graphs, bed by now a bond
more secure than sheets simply bespangled,
lickety split. As you slept, like a zealot,
I counted the coinage of your eyes, your
stuffed purses rummaged by REM, and I wanted
to seize your dream, reach in, change you. A ration
of me you own, the bit indivisible.
Betting love's no law of averages,
morning no penny to be pinched back.

3. Because I Wouldn't Ever Kill You

Forgive me. Last night I lay awake trying
to learn the language of your breath. At times,
I'd swear I heard your wind's idiom, a whiff's
grammar and grace, the figure eight only
your body can stencil in air. The clock boxed
off 2:00, then 3:00. I envied oxygen's
blocks, their making motion inmost into you,
knew never was enough made of one wind
warmed in that declension which is yours, twinned,
flushed luck of lung sacs. I wish I could stop
listening for the secret which is wholly
yours. Or ever forget to praise that air's
invisible essay, this love for how a breeze,
once held, can hold you, and still be free.

4. Beguilement

Sometimes the thud of bee falling,
sometimes a short fast flight
into the light-filled limits
of its world.
Her body, in sickness and in health.
His body, in sickness and in health.
Somewhere the hive, invisible,
little buzzing tenants hell-bent on
promise. Contract, home, a shape
of wadded paper forcing them one way then another,
relentless.
And for years, cruelties
chewed over, until not to touch
was its own tenderness.
Also the flesh no longer
a wall they could count on.
Still, kindness in the house
and on the table, the ochre and scorched
black bodies, each hard carapace
not let to die, the sprawl
of distances to marry again and again
a scent of bread   *I do*
with honey and sting   *I will*
heat blasting the room, their faces damp, going gold
as they opened the doors, letting the creature, all
float and tremble, free.

Narcissus and the Aquarium Guide

Truth to tell, he was for floods
Of love long due, since lapped
At him always the model lake's
Waves in verge, arriving
Whipstitched, bent
With hunger. I saw him first
At noon. Having riddled his hips
Through turnstyle, he stood
Nearby my asides until all
Inwardly I sat, stoved.
A bilge and paste
Of appellation I gave
Him: prickle back
Eel, gunnel, and rockweed,
The back-lit scrod
Schooling in cathedral.
He found the glass
Miraculous, came often.
How dully I lusted
For his point of view,
Unpierceable, felt his glance
Briefly as fins float
Upright in agar. Is as does,
Turns out, in beauty, fubbing,
As always, its own
Reflection al-
Chemical. Came
The detritus, of course,
When he stopped coming.
By day's end, after crowds
And hours, children screeching
More time at the touch pool,
I tried to teach how it takes

One anemone, splitting,
Asexual, *some real work*,
To get up, walk away from itself.

Hippocampus

1.

"Remember me? Think sputum
threaded to spud, a root-bulb coiffed
across cortex. Think split

in fissure without whom who's to hold down
brain's duff and dander,
your forest floor.

If you say pillars in the skull-
case you can't feel it.
Now

feel it. Such time as you bent down
for him in the tight blue dress, that first being
seen.

Like Mother in tuck mode, the beautiful,
a snoot full, the good electric booze full,
also

the air she spun to gold. Look how the actual
fattens. A certain debit echoes, plumbing
the footstep below

first print, slime trail
of cerebellum, endless anatomies
of ooze.

As for the you and not-you creeping in,
more jetsam and flop, anciently naked.
Take

the way a train whistle becomes
midnight meeting, a cat's
                    howl,

mostly, climbing into your bed. Sing praise.
Sing *I was hewn down at the wood's edge*
                    (love), *taken from my stump.*"

2.

So I woke up finally, pure luck, the when of it, saw
door jimmied open, cabinets ajar, windows
gap-toothed wide. Stood there naked,
all the openings I call my own in that moment

> *Upon arriving at the brain with its membranes*
> *the skull-cap must be removed*

As if new world, as if spun from. Then I remembered getting up
for the cone of light bursting gold into bedroom.
Air I guess, shoving its elbows in,
little hallway filled with what animals, men, more wind in between

> *The bone snaps easily with hammer and chisel*

And had another second gone by back then I'll bet
all the burglars inside the bedroom, the bed, me,
everyone scraping for my name before my name
because I happened to be

> *Here the student must be precise*
> *lifting one inch above the margin or orbit*

there so I must have startled them slamming the first door and later
all quicksilver timing at the base of my brain
beginning the scream

> *Loosen frame with fingers, detach*
> *the once many firing ganglia*

So you see, one time the instant
split wide open
enough to make me believe in angels

3.

Because he wanted to see it all, he climbed
the nine times nine stones, a stair of lucky number.
Path to slough off worldly feet. Side-stepping, in fact,
trash—the spent fruit, apple cores, grape stems dropped
by others. After a while he could hear the market's
croon far below, its cry of flutes and crotch for sale.
And when the line rushes back to him, *how this middle
earth fails and falls,*
                         more red dust pesters his open
eyes, mouth, ears, all the vein tracks coursing to brain.

Later at the peak, he can see altar smoke rising, ash-
flaked laughter, palms of the many lifted up. Also,
all around the relic, pillars of air and light
body up the temple's one gold skull.
                             It's only crossing
to the other side he finds, for the first time,
offerings stacked with care, the rinds of jackfruit
or carcass charred, left out, heads of fallen animals
in there. As if the ant-tracked, fly-trod flesh could let
him feel what he came here to feel, a breaking
bruise by bruise, his own face
fissured open for this knowing and not
knowing.

The Post Sublime

Because I said nothing of the Nutria,
cousin to beaver or sloppy muskrat,
western bred then forgotten for its fur,
who died by the edge of the road so that I
could find, skin stripped clean by traffic,
the jawbone and take it home and set its teeth,
intact, on the bedside table to keep me
mindful of the hard enamels of hunger.
Because I turned neither right nor left
for the border scrim of sight where must
have been, all season: the sudden
cross-stitchings of the finches, the ant
who carried its brother across a stone.
Yesterday, the local hawk, mateless,
flew into himself, trying wildly
with his talons for the too steep ledge
of my window. I saw the quick head, beak,
breast go storm, then the feathered
slam up into the limits of the wrongly seen.
His wanting to cross the span of sky
and glass, sky and else. Now I keep his eye
in mind, his coming up close to look harder in
with steady yellow stare, before falling
and wings, his throwing the air more open.

More Scenes From a Body

As for that field, mud-rutted, a stammer
of leaves let go, its center
hollowed for skateboards to ride

                      cement ridge and spray-painted contour,
I remember how the best of them,
a red-head, could come out of hunch

and upswing to find the single lift
he'd trust: the well-timed leap, before
the board, back kicked, floated free

                          into his hand, cupped and waiting.
Life itself, for me, though I was half
drunk in those days, wasting whole

hours with all eight as they wheeled, circled
round, lined up, rolled down. After a few
drinks I thought I could see, full

                     speed, the greater gravity they got
on under curve, added weight they needed
to feel some baseline

of the body—small faith
that fell again and again that winter,
filling the white air between us.

Though not for the going only, I'd say, this girl
spun makeshift as Sargent made her
in *El Jaleo*: dance where she's about

        to drop-kick all the footlights, fling
her own shadow, ramshackle, up
the paint and oil of a barroom wall.

Also to get there, aimed off stage.
Edge of her left hand, raised, hell
bent on elsewhere. Until no one

        cares how the air's thickened
to visible, smoke and charcoals swilling the small
room round. Since it's always her good

move they need—her *now* and
now—leading us past paint's field
and tincture, past the lesser fidgets

        of image. Top of her form. And we want
her all the more, onlookers, coming in closer
for her skirts caught in eddy, her color of

salt-blear-on-sea-rock,
that fulcrum. Everyone drunk. Everyone
on edge. See how the others, stage

        right, claw inwardly up their own
arms, how the men down left strum
guitars all the harder. And if, outside

the frame, what little
light there is loosens like a syntax,
she'd push them all out there,

        spin the flash and pivot of their wishes,
the living—each and every—
hauled fast into the black.

Tell me it all comes down
to your arm flung out, 3 a.m., its breaking
just across my belly, this proof absolute

I'm no one and nowhere else.
Happens that I'd like to touch
the waves your closed eyes ride in sleep,

your bit of dream beneath
the dumb show: lash, outer lid,
REM twitch. Awake, I'd make you see

how our room spins
its ink pools in ash, how these shadows
and passing headlights keep slipping

right into the endlessly under—
until *river*'s the word I'd whisper.
Then *bed*, the deeper beneath it.

And still you sleep like a child, like the one
in raw daylight we try lately to make from our bodies.
I can't help wondering who said it's so much better,

to be
alive, to add, from our openings, another
flesh?

Wall's edge,
the dark-on-darks tunnel
down to some sunken ground

we'll never see. God: I wish

you'd wake up. Listen—the early
risers slam their doors, off to work. Listen—

              the pin-in-place, the one, somewhere
already itself, little shadow leaving
shadow to step on stage—can't you hear

it?—the meanings getting heavier
with the green and give,
eyes closed, scrawled with our singular

                   mistakes, having to come down from
ghostling to fingers to first breath to us,
and we two growing into its first fat story.

Wake up, heart, it's coming, losing
the tracks it took to get here, ready for a name,
palms opening, ready to hand it all over—

Notes

"Last Score": A few details regarding Robert Schumann's last meal before seeing Clara Schumann for the final time are taken from *Clara Schumann: The Artist and the Woman* by Nancy B. Reich.

"Bird of Paradise Aubade With Bangkok Etching Over the Bed": The art piece referred to is a temple rubbing in chalk, now often sold to tourists, depicting a scene from the *Ramakien*, the Thai version of the Indian *Ramayana*. In it, the hero's consort, Nang Sida, abducted by a rival lover, is set free. The poem is dedicated to my husband, Andrew Feld.

"His Sepulchre in Two Voices": In part, this poem was inspired by Piero Della Francesca's *Resurrection*, depicting the moment of Christ's emergence from the tomb when it is surrounded by guards who have fallen asleep. The painting is in San Sepulcro.

"A Vision of St. Clare": The poem depicts a legend of Saint Clare in which she takes leave of her parents' house as a young girl by dismantling the "door" through which the dead were carried from the premises on their way to burial. Another account tells of her secret meetings with Saint Francis during the night.

"Chronicles of the Price of Light": Section 2 is loosely based on my reading of William D. Nordhaus' article entitled "Do Real-Output and Real-Wage Measure Capture Reality?" as reprinted in *The Economics of New Goods* (University of Chicago Press, 1997). Many thanks to my father, Jack Triplett, for directing me to the article in the first place. Section 4 takes its title from the book of essays by the same name by Salman Rushdie, and is dedicated to Ba Pao. Section 5 contains two middle stanzas which are written in a traditional Thai form called *kap yanii*. In it the lines of four are broken into two parts consisting of five and six syllables each. The fifth syllable must rhyme with the eighth syllable of the first line. The last syllable of the first line must also rhyme with the fifth of the second, while the second line's final syllable must rhyme again with the last syllable of the third line, and so on, repeating the internal fifth and eighth syllable pattern as well.

"Hive": This poem is dedicated to the poet Doug Larsen.

"Whether To Marry": The poem refers at several junctures to *The Merchant of Venice*, especially the riddle game of inscribed caskets to which Portia's suitors are subjected.

"Grief Hotline": A version of the poem's narrative was suggested to me by Jonathan Wilks. It is dedicated to him.

"Hippocampus": The source of some details, with liberal re-wording, is *Gray's Anatomy*. The italicized lines in Section 1 are from "The Dream of the Rood," an anonymous tenth-century poem in which the cross as wooden object speaks of its own transformation. The lines remembered in Section 3 are from "The Wanderer," in which the hero in exile speaks to himself.

Pimone Triplett is also the author of *Ruining the Picture* (Northwestern/ Triquarterly, 1998), which won the Hazel Hall Poetry Award. She holds an MFA from the Iowa Writer's Workshop, and has done graduate work at the University of Houston. Her work has been widely published and anthologized, appearing in *Agni; New England Review; The Paris Review; Poetry; Triquarterly; Yale Review; American Poetry: The Next Generation; Asian American Poetry, The Next Generation;* and *The New American Poets, A Bread Loaf Anthology*. She is of Thai-American descent. Currently teaching in the MFA Program at the University of Oregon, she has also taught in the Warren Wilson College MFA Program for Writers. She lives in Eugene and is married to the poet Andrew Feld.